International Powerlifters Council

Originally founded to create a powerlifting organization / family for Combat Veterans unable to leave their home due to PTSD challenges, the International Powerlifters Council, LLC has grown to include members from many different areas around the World, whether they're military or civilian. Some are unable to leave their homes due to PTSD issues while others are unable to attend meets due to financial challenges.

Our goal is to provide a friendly and welcoming environment to any person who has chosen powerlifting as a personal development sport / hobby in their life. *Visit:* InternationalPowerliftersCouncil.com

Page Intentionally Left Blank

Powerlifting 101

For All Genders - Adults & Youth!

Brian K Allen

Page Intentionally Left Blank

CERTIFIED APEX FITNESS PROFESSIONAL

Be it known that the faculty of the Apex Fitness Group has confirmed that

Brian Allen

has successfully completed the Apex Fitness Professional Certification and the comprehensive examination required to obtain certification as an Apex Fitness Professional.

In testimony whereof the Seal of the Apex Fitness Group is affixed.

CPT-331504
Certificate Number

10/27/06
Expiration Date

President & CEO

Director of Education

Brian K. Allen, 2014

Page Intentionally Left Blank

Copyright Page

ISBN-13: 978-1537609379

ISBN-10: 1537609378

First CreateSpace printing, September 10, 2016

Page Intentionally Left Blank

Page Intentionally Left Blank

Dedication

This book is dedicated to my brother Brock Allen, and friends John Ogradny, Alfredo Richards, and Chris Padilla. When I think of going to the gym, I think of you fellas. Pushing steel in our teenage & young adult years, is among the best memories of my life.

I've never been a competitive lifter but my love for powerlifting is largely in part to the friendship and brotherhood, each of you, provided me at various times of my life. Thank you.

Page Intentionally Left Blank

Acknowledgements

To Jimmy Verdon *(NFL, CFL, and of course, ASU ☺).* We clocked a lot of hours working together. From talking about family & children, to goofing off, to discussing life… it was always fun. One thing I always was impressed by was your in-depth knowledge of strength & power. I've seen your programs for young kids… as well as the incredibly complex strength training program you created for college level athletes. *(Those spreadsheets were intense! lol)* You're a true professional… and from this guys perspective, a great Dad!

Jimmy Verdon   Brian Allen

Page Intentionally Left Blank

Table of Contents

Page Intentionally Left Blank

Chapter 1

Why I Love

&

Recommend Powerlifting

No citizen has a right to be an amateur in the matter
of physical training… what a disgrace it is for a man
to grow old without ever seeing the beauty and
strength of which his body is capable.

~ Socrates

Powerlifting has been a part of my world in some way or another, my entire life. My first introduction to the term itself, came from my Dad, after I asked him, "How did you get so strong?". He was always the strong one / tough guy among the adults. Of course, I'm biased. But that's truly, what I remember.

Unfortunately, I didn't get his genetics. My brother did though! Brock is strong as hell. Deadly grip above all else. Back to Dad though. Here are two pics of him, side-by-side.

On left, he was 20 years old I believe. On the right, 67 years old. He was of a funny generation. Pick things up, put them down. "Oh that? That looks like a ¼ in varicose vein. It popped out during a squat." or "Oh that? Probably just a hernia." Dad, think you should get that looked at? "Nah. Not this week. I will if it begins to bug me though." And the best one ever was at a Doctor appointment. One day they did xrays, ekg's, etc. looking at his heart. The Dr. put the images on the wall, and asked him, "How long ago were these two heart attacks? My dad told the Dr., "I've never had a heart attack."

The Dr. said, "Mr. Allen – see this black area of your heart? That was your first heart attack. See this dark grey area? That was your second heart attack." My dad says, "Well, nobody told me I had a heart attack!". He was pissed at the Dr. – unreal! His statements will live forever, and bring a smile to his kids and grandkids… forever. He's since passed away, but just like most dads, to their sons… he was my hero.

So I grow up a little, and decided I like wrestling. My dad was like, "oh helllllll… you need to start lifting weights Brian". I was the skinny kid in the house and he knew what kinda trouble I was asking for. So, there I began lifting… in 5th grade.

He also told me how important mentors were. He said, "Brian, you need to find and follow mentors and coaches for different things in life. I'm your dad, and of course I hope I can be your coach for most things. But only you will know if you're getting what you need from me. So, if it's not me, maybe it can be Paul (the neighbor guy across the street), or Gary (a cousin of my mom). Pick them carefully and make sure they have already accomplished whatever you're looking to accomplish."

That was a huge moment for me. In my life, my mentors came in the form of wrestling coaches, martial art instructors, weight club coaches (Jr High & High School), military supervisors, and strength coaches (in my adult years).

If you'll allow – **I'd like to be your powerlifting coach.** You see, all of the knowledge & guidance in the book isn't of my own creation. The knowledge was given to me by my mentors. I paid a lot financially however. ACE & APEX certifications and re-certs every two years. Strength seminars, books, and DVD's. The one thing I always felt was missing, was a focus on "normal people". Most books, seminars, and dvds focused only on competitive powerlifting. Fitness trainers at the gym were incredibly expensive and honestly, seem to put every client through a cookie-cutter "Balance & Core" routine for the first month or two. These people spent a lot of money and from my observation… weren't getting the value they should have.

So, for under $20, **I hope this book will "sell you" on powerlifting.** I hope you make it part of your lifestyle and reap the rewards it has given me. I've never competed. My need for powerlifting was to enhance my martial art training, so that I could make it home alive. I've worked in the executive protection (bodyguard) industry my entire life. I've used powerlifting to prepare for the job… and also during rehabilitation, when I was injured. If you do attend competitions, you'll find athletes that range from 13 – 75 years old! It's truly an activity for all ages & genders.

So, if you're ready – let's move on to chapter one!

Chapter 2

History Of Powerlifting

It wasn't until my late twenties that I learned
that by working out I had given myself a great
gift. I learned that nothing good comes
without work and a certain amount of pain.

~ Henry Rollins

I'm so excited to write this book. After more than 25 years of weight training, aimed at enhancing my performance at work *(military police, executive protection, martial art instructor)*, It's been my experience and observation that power lifting is arguably the best option, among the weight training sports. The other two being Olympic weightlifting and bodybuilding. So yes, I'm biased. I've observed too many injuries in Olympic weightlifting and seen too many unhealthy bodybuilders to sway my opinion. But hey, it's just one man's opinion. ☺

What specifically is Powerlifting? It's a strength sport that consists of three attempts, at maximal weight, on three lifts. Those lifts are:

- squat
- bench press
- deadlift

However, some federations also include an additional test of strength -- the strict barbell curl. Depending on the federation in question, the strict curl is an optional extra or is added to the normal squat, bench press and deadlift competition. To ensure every competitor's performance is comparable, the strict curl is governed by rules.

Powerlifting evolved from a sport known as "odd lifts", which followed the same three-attempt format. However, these contests used a wider variety of events, similar to today's strongman competitions. Eventually, odd lifts became standardized to the current three.

How far back does the sport go? The roots of powerlifting are in traditions of strength training stretching back as far as Greek and Roman times. The modern sport originated in the United States and the UK in the 1950s. Previously, the weightlifting governing bodies in both countries had recognized various 'odd lifts' for competition and record purposes. During the 1950s, Olympic weightlifting declined in the United States, while strength sports gained many new fans.

In 1958, the AAU's National Weightlifting Committee decided to begin recognizing records for 'odd lifts'. The first genuine national 'meet' was held in September 1964 under the auspices of the York Barbell Company. Ironically, Bob Hoffman, the owner of York Barbell, had been a long-time adversary of the sport. But his company was now making powerlifting equipment to make up for the sales it had lost on Olympic-style equipment. *Funny how money-things like that, can change our opinions, right?* ☺

During the late 1950s and early 1960s various 'odd lift' events gradually developed into the specific lifts – the bench press, the squat, and the deadlift and lifted in that order. Bob Hoffman became more and more influential in the development of this new lifting sport and organized 'The Weightlifting Tournament of America' in 1964 - effectively the first US National championships. In 1965, the first named USA National Championships were held.

During the same period, lifting in Britain also had factions. In the late 1950s, and because the ruling body *(BAWLA)* were only interested in the development of Olympic lifting, a breakaway organization called the Society of Amateur Weightlifters had been formed to cater for the interests of lifters who were not particularly interested in doing Olympic lifting.

Although at that time there were 42 recognized lifts, the "Strength Set" *(Biceps Curl, Bench Press, and Squat)* soon became the standard competition lifts, and both organizations held Championships on these lifts *(as well as on the Olympic lifts)* until 1965. In 1966, the Society of Amateur Weightlifters re-joined BAWLA and, in order to fall into line with the American lifts, the Curl was dropped and replaced with the Deadlift.

The first British Championship was held in 1966. During the late 60's and at the beginning of the 70's, various friendly international contests were held. At the same time, in early November of each year and to commemorate Bob Hoffman's birthday, a prestige lifting contest was always held as part of "Bob Hoffman's Birthday Party." In 1971, it was decided to make this event the "World Weightlifting Championships." The competitors were predominantly a whole bunch of American lifters, plus four from Great Britain and one from the West Indies. All the Referees were American. This event was held in York, Pennsylvania, on Saturday 6 November 1971.

Weights were in pounds. The lifting order was called the 'rising bar' system. This was long before the Rounds system. The first lift was the Bench Press. There was no such thing as bench shirts or squat suits, and various interpretations were held regarding the use of and length of knee wraps and weightlifting belts.

Obviously, the lack of formalized rules resulted in some disputes. But check this out! At the 'first' World Championships, one of the American Super heavyweights, Jim Williams *(nicknamed 'Chimes')* benched 660 lbs on a second attempt *(no shirt)*.

Some other notable lifts – Larry Pacifico benched 515 lbs, and John Kuc deadlifted 820 lbs. Hugh Cassidy and Williams both totaled 2,160 lbs. Cassidy got the win, because of a lower bodyweight in the Super heavyweight division.

In 1972 the 'second' AAU World Championships were held on November 10th & 11th . This time, there were 8 lifters from Great Britain, six Canadians, two Puerto Ricans, three Zambians, and one from the West Indies. With 67 lifters in all, the other 47 were Americans. Lifts were still measured in pounds, the bench press was the first lift, and there were still no suits, power belts, or fancy wraps.

Mike Shaw 'lost' his world title, that he had won the previous year, to American Jack Keammerer. Ron Collins made up for his 'bomb' on the bench in '71 and stormed to the 75 kg title. At Super *(over 110 kg)* John Kuc beat Jim Williams with an incredible 2,350 lbs total *(raw)*. Kuc squatting 905 lbs for a record squat and Williams benching a massive 675 lbs - the greatest bench press ever at the time.

The IPF Is Born

The International Powerlifting Federation was formed immediately after the contest, so none of the lifts could be yet registered as official world records. The 1973 Worlds was also held in York, Pennsylvania. This time there were only 47 entrants; 1 from Sweden, 1 from Puerto Rico Peter Fiore – still lifting for Zambia, 2 Canadians, 1 West Indian, 8 from Great Britain, and the rest Americans.

Finally, the officiating became a bit more 'international'; Tony Fitton and Terry Jordan from Britain, a Canadian, and a Zambian, assisting with the Refereeing duties. American Bob Crist was the IPF President, and another American, Clarence Johnson, was Vice-President. 1973 was the first time that the lifts were done in the order we now recognize – Squat, Bench Press, Deadlift. Precious Mackenzie, won his third World title.

1974 was the first time that "teams" had to be selected in advance. With 74 entrants this was the largest Worlds so far. The 52 kg class was introduced – and there were 9 lifters entered. In 1975 the World Championships was held outside America for the first time, in Birmingham, England at the Town Hall, hosted by the legendary Vic Mercer. 82 lifters this time. Unusual for a competition, the Supers lifted first. This was because the Television company filming the event were only interested in filming the 'big guys'.

The establishment of the IPF in 1973 spurred the establishment of the EPF *(European Powerlifting Federation)* in 1974. Since it was closely associated with bodybuilding and women had been competing as bodybuilders for years, the new sport was opened to them very quickly. The first U. S. national championships for women were held in 1978 and the IPF added women's competition in 1979.

In the USA, the Amateur Sports Act of 1978, required that each Olympic or potential Olympic sport, must have its own national governing body by November 1980. As a result, the AAU lost control of virtually every amateur sport. The U.S.P.F. was founded in 1980 as the new national governing body for American powerlifting.

Soon, controversy over drug testing would cause powerlifting to splinter into multiple federations. In 1981, the American Drug Free Powerlifting Association *(ADFPA)*, led by Brother Bennett, became the first federation to break away from the USPF, citing the need to implement effective drug testing in the sport. *(My kinda people!)*

Meanwhile, the IPF was moving towards adopting drug testing at international meets, and requiring member nations to implement drug testing at national meets as well. In 1982, drug testing was introduced to the IPF men's international championship, although the USPF championships that year did not have drug testing. The IPF's push for drug testing was resisted by some American lifters, and in 1982 Larry Pacifico and Ernie Frantz founded the American Powerlifting Federation *(APF)*, which advertised its categorical opposition to all drug testing. *(Insert author "boooooo" here.)*

In 1987 the American Powerlifting Association *(APA)* and World Powerlifting Alliance were formed by Scott Taylor. The APA and WPA offer both drug tested and non-tested categories in most of their competitions. Ultimately, the USPF failed to conform to IPF demands, and was expelled from the international body in 1997, with the ADFPA, now named USA Powerlifting *(USAPL)*, taking its place.

Despite the trend towards more and more federations, each with their own rules and standards of performance, some powerlifters have attempted to bring greater unity to the sport. For example, 100% RAW that promoted unequipped competition merged with another federation, Anti-Drug Athletes United *(ADAU)* in 2013.

The Revolution Powerlifting Syndicate (RPS), founded by Gene Rychlak in 2011, might also be considered a move towards greater unity, as the RPS breaks the tradition of charging lifters membership fees to a specific federation in addition to entry fees for each competition. Also, some meet promoters have sought to bring together top lifters from different federations, outside existing federations' hierarchy of local, regional, national and international meets; a prominent example of this is the Raw Unity Meet *(RUM)*, held annually since 2007.

More Equipment & More Rules

For some reason, bench pressing 500lbs - 600lbs wasn't enough for some people. Others were upset that they could only squat 700lbs. Many were sad they could only deadlift 900lbs. So, being the goofy human beings we are… people began creating supportive equipment. *Can you tell I'm not much of a fan, of this equipment?* ☺

As new equipment was developed, it was another factor used to distinguish powerlifting federations from one another. Weight belts and knee wraps *(originally simple Ace bandages)* predated powerlifting, but in 1983 John Inzer invented the first piece of equipment distinct to powerlifters - the bench shirt.

Bench shirts and squat/deadlift suits *(operating on the same principle)* became popular in powerlifting, but only some federations adopted the latest and most supportive canvas, denim, and multiply polyester designs, while others maintained more restrictive rules on which supportive equipment could be used.

The Monolift, a rack in which the bar catches swing out, eliminating the walkout portion of the squat, was invented by Ray Madden and first used in competition in 1992. This innovation, too, was adopted by some federations and forbidden in others. Other inventions included specialized squat bars and deadlift bars, moving away from the IPF standard, of using the same bar, for all three lifts.

The rules of powerlifting have also evolved and differentiated. For example, in ADFPA/USAPL competition, the "press" command on the bench press was used for a while, not used, and then used again, following a 2006 IPF motion to reinstate this rule. IPF rules also mandate a "start" command at the beginning of the bench press.

Many other federations, for example the Natural Athlete Strength Association *(NASA)*, have never used the "start" command. As a further example of diversifying rules of performance, in 2011 the Southern Powerlifting Federation *(SPF)* eliminated the "squat" command at the beginning of the squat. Some federations also now allow the sumo variation of the deadlift, which varies with the feet being considerably wider apart and some tension taken off the lower spine being taken up by the legs. Many communities and federations however do not class the sumo variation as a technical deadlift.

Chapter 3

The Evolution Of
Supportive Equipment

To keep the body in good health is a duty,
otherwise we shall not be able to keep
our mind strong and clear.

~ Buddha

In powerlifting, supportive equipment refers to items like:

- supportive shirts
- briefs
- suits
- knee wraps

These items are made of materials that store elastic potential energy and thereby assist the three lifts contested in the sport: squat, bench press and deadlift. Personally, I think these things are unneeded for competition. Here's a piece that is written on our website at InternationalPowerliftersCouncil.com

We embrace "RAW" & Drug-Free Powerlifting. Basically, the only equipment we like to see is a 3 – 4 inch weightlifting belt. No bench shirts, body suits, hand / wrist wraps around a bar, excessive knee wraps, etc.

Listen, if I have so much weight on the bench press bar that my shoulders will explode... then it's too much weight for me. I'm not strong enough to bench press that weight.

If I have so much weight on the squat rack that my knees will explode... then it's too much weight for me. I'm not strong enough to squat that weight.

If I have so much weight on the dead-lift platform that the bar slips out of my hands... then it's too much weight for me. I'm not strong enough to dead-lift that weight.

Many lifters disagree with me on the topic, and that's ok. The main point I want to make is that people who train, should be proud of their natural strength gains. Being a strong human is pretty cool. I personally don't see the pride in using equipment that makes me stronger. It's not ME. It's actually cheating in my mind. *Obviously for rehabilitation and other medical reasons, I support the use of equipment.* Supportive equipment is a large topic of discussion and practice in the world of powerlifting, so let's continue on with the topic.

The use of supportive equipment distinguishes 'equipped' and 'un-equipped' or 'raw' divisions in the sport, and 'equipped' and 'unequipped' records in the competition lifts. The wide differences between equipped and unequipped records in the squat and bench suggest that supportive equipment confers a substantial advantage to lifters in these disciplines. This is less evident in the case of the deadlift, where the lack of an eccentric component to the lift minimizes how much elastic energy can be stored in a supportive suit.

Supportive equipment should not be confused with the equipment on which the lifts are performed, such as a bench press bench or the barbell and weight plates. The same thing goes for personal accessories such as a weightlifting belt that may allow greater weight to be lifted, but by mechanisms other than storing elastic energy.

Equipped Powerlifting Meets

Equipped lifters compete separately from raw lifters. Equipped lifters will wear a squat suit, knee wraps, a bench shirt, and a deadlift suit. These four things, are the things that separate equipped lifters and raw lifters. A squat suit is made of an elastic-like material, and a single-ply polyester layer. This allows "pop" out of the hole of a squat, the bottom, and rigidity for the lifter to keep him, or her, upright during the squat allowing the lifters hips to stay underneath them. This allows lifters to lift more weight than they normally could without the suit.

In my humble opinion, the "pop" things I see at some meets and on social media are just dangerous. A pop is when someone unracks the squat bar super hard and/or finishes their squat with an over exaggerated lockout. If you are unracking the bar super hard, you are setting yourself up for injuries *(at worst)* or in a terrible start position *(at best)*. Since a lot of lifters embrace the "pop", I'll include it as we go along.

There are also multi-ply suits giving the lifter even more rigidity, like that of a traditional canvas suit, and the same pop as a single-ply suit or briefs. During the squat, lifters also tend to wear knee wraps. Even though knee wraps will be a sub-classification of raw lifting - it will still be worn by equipped lifters. A raw lifter who would squat in knee wraps will have the weight lifted noted as "in wraps" to distinguish this from the other raw lifters. Knee wraps are made out of the same, or very similar, elastic material as wrist wraps are made out of.

They are wrapped around the lifters knees very tightly with the lifter usually not being able to do it himself and needing someone to assist them in doing so. The knee wraps are wrapped in a spiral or diagonal method. The knee wraps build elastic energy during the eccentric part of the squat and once the lifter has hit proper depth the lifter will start the concentric part of the movement releasing this elastic energy and using it to help them move the weight upwards. It gives the lifter more spring, or pop out of the hole of the squat resulting in a heavier and faster squat.

For the bench press, there are also single-ply and multi-ply bench shirts, that work similarly to a squat suit. It acts as "artificial pectoral muscles and shoulder muscles" for the lifter. It resists the movement of the bench press by compressing and building elastic energy. When the bar is still and the official gives the command to press the compression and elastic energy of the suit aids in the speed of the lift, and support of the weight that the lifter would not be able to provide for himself without the bench shirt. In order to achieve proper tightness and fitting the lifter must be assisted when putting the bench shirt on because it's just not possible to be done alone.

For the deadlift suit, there is single-ply and multi-ply as well. The elastic energy is built when the lifter goes down to set up and place their grip on the bar before lifting even starts. The deadlift suit aids in getting the weight off the floor, considered to be the first part of the movement, but not very helpful on the lockout portion of the deadlift, known as the second part of the movement.

Principles of Operation

As you can now see, supportive equipment is used to increase the weight lifted in powerlifting exercises. It's really a snug garment that is worn over a joint or joints *(such as the shoulders or hips)*. This garment deforms during the downward portion of a bench press or squat, or the descent to the bar in the deadlift, storing elastic potential energy. On the upward portion of each lift, the elastic potential energy is transferred to the barbell as kinetic energy, aiding in the completion of the lift.

Some claim that supportive equipment prevents injuries by compressing and stabilizing the joints over which it worn. For example, the bench shirt is claimed to support and protect the shoulders. Critics point out that the greater weights used with supportive equipment and the equipment's tendency to change the pattern of the movement may compromise safety, as in the case of the bar moving towards the head during the upward portion of the shirted bench press.

Yada, yada, yada. You know what else prevents injuries? Lowering the weight to an amount the athlete can actually lift! There I go talking smack again.

Material and Construction

Different materials are used in the construction of supportive equipment. Squat suits may be made of varying types of polyester, or of canvas. Canvas is less elastic, and therefore considered to provide greater 'stopping power' at the bottom of the movement but less assistance with the ascent. Bench shirts may be made of polyester or denim, where the denim again provides a less-elastic alternative to the polyester.

Knee wraps are made of varying combinations of cotton and elastic. Supportive equipment can be constructed in different ways to suit lifters' preferences. A squat or deadlift suit may be constructed for a wide or a narrow stance; and a bench shirt may be constructed with 'straight' sleeves *(perpendicular to the trunk of the lifter)* or sleeves that are angled towards the abdomen.

The back of the bench shirt may be closed or open, and the back panel may or may not be of the same material as the front of the shirt. Similarly, 'hybrid' squat suits can include panels made from canvas and polyester, in an effort to combine the strengths of each material. When two or more panels overlay one another in a piece of supportive equipment, that equipment is described as 'multi-ply', in contrast to 'single-ply' equipment made of one layer of material throughout.

Page Intentionally Left Blank

Chapter 4

Raw Powerlifting

*Training gives us an outlet for suppressed
energies created by stress and thus
tones the spirit just as exercise
conditions the body.*

~ Arnold Schwarzenegger

Unequipped or "RAW" powerlifting has been codified in response to the proliferation and advancement of bench shirts and squat/deadlift suits. The AAU first began its raw division in 1994 and the term "raw" was apparently coined by Al Siegal. Siegal later formed the ADAU in 1996. The 100% RAW federation was founded in 1999. Within a decade, many established federations have come to recognize "raw" divisions in addition to their traditional *(open)* divisions permitting single-ply or multi-ply equipment.

During this time frame however, RAW lifting was looked upon as a beginners stage by the elite lifters in powerlifting. In January 2008, the Raw Unity Meet *(simply known as "RUM")* was formed by Eric Talmant and Johnny Vasquez. This meet was really the turning point in raw lifting. It was a crucial contest that gathered the best lifters under one roof regardless of gear worn to compete without equipment. Athletes such as Brian Schwab, Amy Weisberger, Beau Moore, Tony Conyers, Arnold Coleman and Dave Ricks were among the first Elite lifters to remove their equipment and compete raw. RUM spearheaded raw lifting into what it has become today.

The United Powerlifting Association *(UPA)* established a standard for raw powerlifting in 2008 and USAPL held the first Raw Nationals in the same year. Eventually, IPF recognized raw lifting with the sanction of a "Classic 'Unequipped' World Cup" in 2012. The IPF then published its own set of standards for raw lifting. By this time, the popularity of raw lifting has surged to the point where raw lifters came to predominate over equipped lifters in local meets.

Because the different rules aren't confusing enough, the IPF's use of the word 'classic' to describe raw powerlifting is differentiated from most other powerlifting federations' use of the word. To differentiate between 'classic raw' and 'modern raw'... classic raw is still unequipped but allows the use of knee wraps while modern raw allows knee sleeves at most. The IPF does not allow knee wraps in its unequipped competitions and would thus be considered 'modern raw' but the IPF does not recognize the word 'raw.' *Having to memorize numerous things like this, can cause me to drink. Often.* ☺

The use of knee sleeves in unequipped powerlifting has brought about much debate as to whether certain neoprene knee sleeves can actually assist a lifter during the squat. Some lifters purposely wear knee sleeves which are excessively tight and have been known to use plastic bags and have others to assist them get their knee sleeves on. This led to the IPF mandating that lifters put on their knee sleeves unassisted.

General Training Information

Weight training routines used in powerlifting are extremely varied. For example, some methods call for the use of many variations on the contest lifts, while others call for a more limited selection of exercises and an emphasis on mastering the contest lifts through repetition.

While many powerlifting routines invoke principles of sports science, such as the "specific adaptation to imposed demand" *(SAID principle)*, there is some controversy around the scientific foundations of particular training methods, as exemplified by the debate over the merits of "speed work," or training to attain maximum acceleration of submaximal weights.

In addition to weight training, powerlifters also pursue other forms of training to improve their performance. For example, aerobic exercise may be used to improve endurance during drawn-out competitions and support recovery from weight training sessions. Yes, cardio training is needed. The first time you knock out a big deadlift workout... and almost pass out... you'll experience why cardiorespiratory health & efficiency is so important.

Common "set & rep" routines are based on a percentage of the lifter's 1RM *(1 Rep Maximum)*. For example, 5 sets of 5 reps *(5x5)* at 75% of the 1RM. Rest periods between sets range from 2–5 minutes based on the lifter's ability to recover fully for the next set.

Chapter 5

The Squat

Everybody wants to be a bodybuilder,
but don't nobody wanna lift no
heavy ass weight.
~ Ronnie Coleman

The squat starts with the lifter standing erect and the bar loaded with weights resting on the lifter's shoulders. At the referee's command, the squat begins. The lifter creates a break in the hips, bends his knees and drops into a squatting position with the hip crease *(the top surface of the leg at the hip crease)* below the top of the knee. The lifter then returns to an erect position. At the referee's command, the bar is returned to the rack and the lift is completed.

Breaking Things Down

After removing the bar from the racks, while facing the front of the platform, the lifter may move forward or backward to establish the lifting position. The top of the bar not more than 3 cm below the top of the anterior deltoids. The bar shall be held horizontally across the shoulders with the hands and/or fingers gripping the bar, and the feet flat upon the platform with the knees locked.

The lifter shall wait in this position for the head referee's signal. The signal will be given as soon as the lifter is set and demonstrates control, with the bar properly positioned. The head referee's signal shall consist of a downward movement of the arm and audible command "Squat".

Upon receiving the head referee's signal, the lifter must bend the knees and lower the body until the top surface of the legs at the hip joint is lower than the top of knees.

The lifter must recover at will, without double bouncing, to an upright position with the knees locked. The bar may stop, but there must be no downward motion during recovery. As soon as the lifter demonstrates a controlled final position, the head referee will give the signal indicating completion of the lift and to replace the bar.

The signal to replace the bar will consist of a backward motion of the arm and the audible command "Rack". The lifter must then make a reasonable attempt to return the bar to the racks. *Below are some more specifics.*

1. The lifter shall face the front of the platform, towards the head referee.

2. The lifter shall not hold the collars or discs at any time during the performance of the lift. However, the edge of the hands gripping the bar may be in contact with the inner surface of the collar.

3. Not more than five and not less than two loaders/spotters shall be on the platform at any time.

4. The lifter may enlist the help of spotters in removing the bar from the racks; however, once the bar has cleared the racks, the spotters shall not physically assist the lifter with regards to actually getting into the proper set position. The spotters may assist the lifter to maintain control should the lifter stumble or demonstrate any evident instability.

5. The lifter will be allowed only one commencement signal per attempt.

6. The lifter may be given an additional attempt at the same weight at the head referee's discretion if failure in an attempt was due to any error by one or more of the spotters.

Causes For "No Lift" (Disqualification)

1. Failure to observe the head referee's signals at the commencement or completion of a lift.

2. Double bouncing or more than one recovery attempt at the bottom of the lift.

3. Failure to assume an upright position with knees locked at the commencement and completion of the lift.

4. Movement of the feet laterally, backward or forward that would constitute a step or stumble.

5. Failure to bend the knees and lower the body until the surface of the legs at the hip joint is lower than the tops of the knees.

6. Any resetting of the feet after the squat signal.

7. Contact with the bar by the spotters between the referee's signals.

8. Contact of elbows or upper arms with the legs.

9. Failure to make a reasonable attempt to return the bar to the racks.

10. Any intentional dropping or dumping of the bar.

Page Intentionally Left Blank

Chapter 6

The Bench Press

One of the greatest experiences in life is achieving
personal goals that others said would be, 'impossible
to attain.' Be proud of your success and share
your story with others.

~ Robert Cheeke

With the lifters' back resting on the bench, the lifter presses the loaded bar, off the rack, at arm's length. The lifter lowers the bar to the chest. When the bar becomes motionless on the chest, the referee gives a "press" command, and the lifter presses it up. Then the referee will call 'Rack' and the lift is completed as the weight is returned to the rack.

Breaking Things Down

1. The front of the bench must be placed on the platform facing the head referee.

2. The lifter must lie backward with shoulders and buttocks in contact with the flat bench surface. The lifter's shoes or toes must be in solid contact with the platform or surface. The position of the head is optional.

3. To achieve firm footing, a lifter of any height may use discs or blocks to build up the surface of the platform. Whichever method is chosen; the shoes must be in a solid contact with the surface. If blocks are used, they shall not exceed 45cm x 45cm.

4. Not more than five and not less than two loaders/spotters shall be in attendance. The lifter may enlist the help of one or more of the designated spotters or enlist a personal spotter in removing the bar from the racks. Only designated spotters may remain on the platform during the lift. The lift off must be to arm's length and not down to the chest. A designated spotter, having provided a center lift-off, must immediately clear the area in front of the head referee and move to either side of the bar. If the personal spotter does not immediately leave the platform area and/or in any way distracts or impedes the head referees' responsibilities, the referees may determine that the

lift is unacceptable, and be declared "no lift" by the referees and given three red lights.

5. The spacing of the hands shall not exceed 81 cm, measured between the forefingers. The bar shall have circumferential machine markings or tape indicating this maximum grip allowance. If the lifter should use an offset or unequal grip on the bar, whereby one hand is placed outside the marking or tape, it is the lifters responsibility to explain this to the head referee, and allow inspection of the intended grip prior to making an attempt. If this is not done until the lifter is on the platform for an official attempt, any necessary explanation and/or measurements will be done on the lifter's time for that attempt. The reverse or underhand grip is forbidden, as is a thumb less grip.

6. After receiving the bar at arm's length, the lifter shall lower the bar to the chest and await the head referees' signal.

7. The signal shall be an audible command "Press" and given as soon as the bar is motionless on the chest. As long as the bar is not so low that it touches the lifter's belt, it is acceptable.

8. The lifter will be allowed only one commencement signal per attempt.

9. After the signal to commence the lift has been given, the bar is pressed upward. The bar shall not be allowed to sink into the chest or move downwards prior to the lifter's attempt to press upward. The lifter will press the bar to straight arm's length and hold motionless until the audible command "Rack" is given. Bar may move horizontally and may stop during the ascent, but may not move downward towards the chest.

Causes For A "No Lift"

1. Failure to observe the referee's signals at the commencement or completion of the lift.

2. Any change in the elected position that results in the buttocks breaking contact with the bench or lateral movement of the hands (between the referee's signals). Any excessive movement or change of contact of the feet during the lift proper.

3. Allowing the bar to sink into the chest after receiving the referee's signal.

4. Pronounced uneven extension of the arms during or at the completion of the lift.

5. Any downward motion of the bar during the course of being pressed out.

6. Contact with the bar by the spotters between the referee's signals.

7. Any contact of the lifter's shoes with the bench or its supports.

8. Deliberate contact between the bar and the bar rest uprights during the lift to assist the completion of the press.

It is the responsibility of the lifter to inform any personally enlisted spotters, to leave the platform as soon as the bar is secured at arm's length. Such spotters shall not return to the platform upon completion or failure of the attempt. It is especially important for a spotter providing a center lift-off to leave the platform quickly so as not to impair the head referee's view. Failure of any personal spotters to leave the platform may cause disqualification of the lift.

Page Intentionally Left Blank

Chapter 7

The Deadlift

Stimulate don't annihilate.

~ Lee Haney

In the deadlift, the athlete grasps the loaded bar which is resting on the platform floor. The lifter pulls the weights off the floor and assumes an erect position. The knees must be locked and the shoulders back, with the weight held in the lifter's grip. At the referee's command, the bar will be returned to the floor under the control of the lifter.

Breaking Things Down

1. The bar must be laid horizontally in front of the lifter's feet, gripped with an optional grip in both hands, and lifted until the lifter is standing erect. The bar may stop but there must be no downward motion of the bar.

2. The lifter shall face the front of the platform.

3. On completion of the lift, the knees shall be locked in a straight position and the lifter shall be standing erect.

4. The head referee's signal shall consist of a downward movement of the arm and the audible command "Down". The signal will not be given until the bar is held motionless and the lifter is in an apparent finished position.

5. Any raising of the bar or any deliberate attempt to do so will count as an attempt.

Causes For A "No Lift"

1. Any downward motion of the bar before it reaches the final position.

2. Failure to stand erect.

3. Failure to lock the knees straight at the completion of the lift.

4. Supporting the bar on the thighs during the performance of the lift. 'Supporting' is defined as a body position adopted by the lifter that could not be maintained without the counterbalance of the weight being lifted.

5. Movement of the feet laterally, backward or forward that would constitute a step or stumble.

6. Lowering the bar before receiving the head referee's signal.

7. Allowing the bar to return to the platform without maintaining control with both hands.

Page Intentionally Left Blank

Chapter 8

Strict Curl

*Those who think they have not time
for bodily exercise will sooner or
later have to find time for illness.*
~ Edward Stanley

The bar used in a strict curl competition is an EZ curl, or cambered, barbell. Most gyms have EZ bars for biceps and triceps training. The camber or bend of the bar provides a comfortable hand and wrist position and also provides a fixed-grip width to ensure all lifters use the same hand placement on the bar. I think the biggest benefit of this bar, is injury prevention. Curling heavy weight on a straight bar has been the cause of numerous wrist injuries. The bar must be held with a double-handed underhand grip with all fingers wrapped around the bar.

Breaking Things Down

Once you have hold of the bar, you must stand completely upright with your knees straight and your arms extended and the bar touching your thighs. While some federations only use judges to confirm the lifter is properly and legally positioned, others federations require the lifter to lean his buttocks and shoulders against a wall or vertical bench.

When the chief judge is happy that you are in the proper starting position, he will give the command "Curl." Without jerking, using your legs or moving your upper body in any way, you should then bend your arms to raise the bar up to your shoulders. At the top of the lift, the judge will give the command "down," which signals that you should lower the bar back to the starting position. Each lifter gets three attempts. The winner is the lifter who successfully curls the heaviest weight.

Causes For A "No Lift"

1. Lifting or lowering the bar before you are instructed to.
2. Moving your feet or bending your knees during the lift
3. Failing to start with your arms fully extended
4. Allowing the bar to travel downward during the lift
5. Lifting the bar unevenly or allowing your butt or back to come away from the wall or bench, if one is being used.

As the exact rules vary from one federation to another. If you are entering a strict curl competition, make sure you check the rules of your specific competition before starting.

Page Intentionally Left Blank

Chapter 9

Powerlifting Injury Prevention

To feel strong, to walk amongst humans with a tremendous feeling of confidence and superiority is not at all wrong. The sense of superiority in bodily strength is borne out by the long history of mankind paying homage in folklore, song and poetry to strong men.

~ Fred Hatfield

Injury prevention is of utmost importance. Not only can injuries take you out of the gym, they can cause you to be unable to work as well. Medical bills plus loss of wages is not a good thing. The overwhelming amount of injuries are preventable. That is a good thing. So, stay focused... use good form... and follow the guidance in this chapter. Rule #1 – talk to your doctor before undertaking any weight training program. What he/she say goes. I can offer global advice, but a doctor is a true expert.

In this chapter, we will be addressing 9 of the most commonly injured areas. To make things easy, we'll discuss them from a top down… or head to toe, manner. We'll look at these areas of the body:

1. Shoulders
2. Chest
3. Back
4. Elbows
5. Wrists
6. Hips
7. Sacroiliac joint
8. Knees
9. Ankles

Each of these areas can be injured during powerlifting. Although injuring a joint such as the knee, while bench pressing, is uncommon… it has still happened. The advice below was given to me by a very experienced powerlifter and RN. So, I'll share it with you!

Shoulders

Shoulder injuries are one of the most common injuries in powerlifting. This is simply because of the anatomy of the shoulder joint and its ability to move more freely than any other joint. There are several different reasons - and ways - that shoulders are injured. Things like shoulder impingement, bursitis, tendon/ligament tears, rotator cuff tears, etc. We will be addressing some of the most common injuries, how they occur, and how to prevent them.

Shoulder Impingement – also known as - subacromialimpingement, swimmer's shoulder, painful arc syndrome, supraspinatus syndrome, and thrower's shoulder. This is a syndrome which occurs when the tendons of the rotator cuff muscles become irritated and inflamed as they pass through the sub acromial space.

This impingement happens for a number of different reasons. Overuse, rounded shoulders, under recovery, and poor circulation can all contribute to shoulder impingement. If you are getting enough sleep, on a sound training program and diet, overuse/under recovery shouldn't be a problem. So that leaves us with poor circulation and rounded shoulders being the main culprit.

These two can easily be corrected. For increasing circulation simply do light rotator cuff exercises before performing bench or any lift involving your shoulders.

Correcting rounded shoulders can take some time, but it is possible by simply training your back/rear deltoids more than you train your chest/shoulders. For every push movement you do, make sure you do a pull movement so you aren't creating a muscle imbalance. In order to correct the rounded shoulders, you're going to want to do more pulling movements. So if you're doing 3 pushing movements, do 4 pulling movements. You can also try some stretches to help with this issue, as well as avoiding slouching in your chair, and maintaining good posture throughout the day.

Bursitis – also known as inflammation or irritation of the bursa. The bursa is a sac filled with lubricating fluid, located between tissues such as bone, muscle, tendons, and skin. Its function is to decrease rubbing, friction, and irritation.

Shoulder bursitis usually happens due to overuse and/or under recovery. It typically happens to people who are benching/overhead pressing several times per week with not enough recovery taking place. This, along with most injuries, is not one that you can "work through". Continuing the motion that aggravated it in the first place, will only make bursitis worse. This may mean taking several months off.

The way to prevent bursitis in the shoulders, is similar to shoulder impingement prehab. Reduce your frequency of the movement that is causing/likely to cause you aggravation. Benching over 3 times per week isn't ideal and will usually lead to an injury like bursitis. Only do what your body can handle. Properly warming up your rotator cuffs, and making sure you don't have any muscle imbalances is also vitally important in preventing bursitis.

Chest

Pectoral strains are probably the most common chest injury. They are usually caused by overuse of the pecs after benching too much. This usually isn't the actual cause of the strain though, the problem is usually a mobility issue, or a technique issue. Flare your elbows and use an extra wide grip and you're pretty much just asking for a pec strain no matter how frequent you bench. It's normally a combination of improper form… and too training sessons per week… that causes pec strains. So, do yourself a favor. Always use good form and be intelligent and strategic with your recuperation days. Strains can also happen from not warming up enough. If you haven't figured it out by now, warming up is extremely important.

Back

People get back pain from all sorts of things, sleeping wrong, bending over wrong, sitting wrong, etc. Trying to pick hundreds of pounds off the ground… puts an immense amount of stress on your body, more specifically your back. Using bad form with heavy weights can destroy a back.

You've probably heard it a million times, but using good form and keeping a straight lower/mid back is absolutely crucial to good back health. You will not be able to make it to the highest levels of powerlifting using bad form. Your body simply won't allow it if you're lifting with incorrect form. Form is everything. More important than competition, is everyday quality of life. Many people benefit from proper powerlifting... people who never have a desire to compete. Why don't they get back injuries? Because they follow the advice in this section!

I'm going to stress properly warming up once again, and also picking up a good 10 mm or 13 mm (thickness) weightlifting belt. If you're planning on competing in powerlifting, go with a four-inch powerlifting belt in either of the above thicknesses. Lighter lifters typically choose the 10 mm, while heavier lifters tend to go with the 13 mm. But it's all up to you. Whatever keeps your guts inside your body. ☺

Elbows

Elbow tendonitis – also known as - tennis elbow. This injury is most commonly caused by overuse.

First things first, cut back on whatever you're doing to cause this pain. Make sure you properly warm up so that your muscles are absorbing the force and not your tendon. Wearing an elbow sleeve or some kind of wrap is a great way to keep your elbow warm, and provide support and compression.

You also can't go wrong with icing your elbows after you work out, and maybe taking an OTC non-steroidal anti-inflammatory drug, or NSAID, such as Ibuprofen or Naproxen. Make sure you take these as often as it says you can on the bottle… to really take full advantage of the anti-inflammatory affects.

Taking these sporadically will not bring down swelling and inflammation as much as taking these consistently throughout the day will.

Be careful though. Excessive NSAID use has been shown to cause liver damage. So only use when necessary. As always, consult your doctor!

Wrists

Wrist injuries typically only affect pressing movements. They can also affect your squat as well. Wrist injuries are mostly caused by lack of a proper warm up and simply lacking flexibility and mobility in the wrist. Using bad form on presses can cause wrist pain. When doing movements such as bench and overhead press, make sure the bar is directly in line with your forearm.

A quick fix for wrist pain is simply wearing wrist wraps on any movement that causes pain or discomfort in the wrist. These can be picked up fairly cheap. However, if you don't want to rely on wrist wraps, you can start by doing some wrist stretches and making sure your wrist joints are fully warmed up before doing any sort of exercise.

Hips

Hip pain is typically caused by lack of mobility, or a posterior weakness. This is also known as, weak glutes or glutes that aren't firing correctly and aren't being utilized to their full extent.

The gluteus maximus is a primary mover of hip extension. Weak glutes mean weak extension. You can see this in lifters when during the eccentric (lowering) phase of the squat they start tipping forward. People talk a lot about core tightness and abdominal bracing as it relates to the forward lean and that's absolutely valid - but also secondary. The first step to maintaining an upright torso is proper eccentric glute control. If you don't have the glute strength to maintain and drive hip extension, then your lower back will kick in to compensate. Something the lower back is not designed to do with the amount of weight powerlifters use.

The three items below will help cure this issue in most cases. Add them to your routine while you simultaneously reduce the amount of weight you're using. A few months of correction can lead to an incredible improvement in your everyday living and of course, your PL total!

1. Pelvic Tilts / Hip Bridges
2. Fire Hydrant / Glute Kick Backs
3. Enhanced stretching for the groin, low back, and glutes.

Sacroiliac Joint

The Sacroiliac Joint, or SI joint, is what connects the spine to the pelvis. It is formed by the connection of the sacrum and the right and left iliac bones. Although this is part of the back, I figured I would give it its own section based on the experiences of many lifters with SI joint injuries.

The SI joint is most commonly injured while deadlifting or squatting. This can be one of the most painful/debilitating injuries, but good news, it's avoidable.

The first thing you should avoid is "form breakdown". Using proper technique is absolutely crucial in powerlifting. All it takes is one sloppy rep, and you could be injured and unable to lift for several months or even the rest of your life. The more weight you're lifting, the more important proper form is. Lighten up on your load until the form is perfect, then start increasing the amount of your weight.

There are also several exercises and stretches you can do to prevent SI joint injuries. If you're already experiencing SI joint pain, it would be a good idea to make these a part of your daily prehab routine.

Knees

One of the most commonly injured joints. Most injuries involve one of the ligaments being sprained. Other injuries such as tendonitis and cartilage tears are also fairly common as well.

Warming up should be your first step to avoiding knee injury. In your overall routine, make sure your posterior muscles are get worked as much as you're working your quads, in order to avoid any muscle imbalances.

You could also try wearing some knee wraps. These will keep your knee warm and provide support/compression.

Ankles

Once you injure your ankle, you are more likely to injure it again compared to someone that has never injured their ankle before.

In addition to properly warming up, there are exercises you can do to increase ankle stability and strength.

Working your tibialis anterior is very important. It's often neglected. This area is activated by flexing your toes – toward your head. Kind of like a reverse calf raise. Go to YouTube, and do a search for tibialis anterior exercise. Hopefully, the video by Anne French is still there. It's so simple! In addition, you should be working your soleus by doing seated calf raises.

Tendon Tears (anywhere in the body)

Tendon tears may seem like an injury that is unavoidable, but that's just not true. The main causes for tendon tears are not warming up properly and improper technique.

When a muscle isn't warmed up enough, or is too tight, it can't effectively absorb the force (weight) that is being placed on it and it then transfers that force to the tendon, and that is when your tendon tears.

This can be prevented by always thoroughly warming up, doing a lot of mobility work, and using correct form / avoiding form breakdown. This means knowing when to call it quits and not trying for that one extra rep. Every single repetition should be completed with perfect form, otherwise you're risking injury.

Knots In Your Muscles

Try using a foam roller, or using a lacrosse ball to break up knots in your muscles, and loosen them up before lifting. Both are very affordable and highly effective.

Chapter 10

Powerlifting Nutrition

Strong people are harder to kill than weak people and more useful in general.

\- Mark Rippetoe

Introduction To Macros and Calories

What does "to macro" mean? "To macro" means tracking the number of grams of protein, carbohydrates, and fats you consume on a particular day. Protein provides us with the raw material needed to build and repair muscle. Fat is needed for hormone production and energy. Carbohydrates are specifically important when it comes to providing our body with energy too. Adequate carbohydrate intake can properly fuel your workouts. Even though powerlifting training doesn't burn many calories, it still places a demand on your body. Also important to remember, although the activity of powerlifting itself doesn't burn many calories… the result of powerlifting *(added muscle)* does burn more calories when resting throughout the day.

This chapter will cover three basic areas. The first section is about what you need to do in order to diet down to a weight class. The second section will cover everything you need to know about gaining the proper amount of weight to move up a weight class. The third and final section will cover gym performance and meet day performance. Just remember, the basics still apply – calories in vs. calories out.

That doesn't change when you're trying to lose weight or gain weight. I believe in flexible dieting and hitting certain amounts of each major macronutrients. It matters much less what you eat but more the amounts… of what you eat. Yes, you can get lean eating ice cream. And yes, you can gain weight from too much grilled chicken and broccoli.

Goal #1 - Dieting Down Into A Weight Class

Remember the goal is the drop fat not muscle. Losing muscle when dieting will make you weaker and leave you feeling fatigued. Dieting down for a weight class takes precision and will power. You have to keep your goal in mind the entire time while dieting, there will be times because your training is so demanding you will be extremely hungry. Fighting off that hunger will leave you leaner and stronger.

Rule No. 1 - Count & Track Your Calories

You need to know how many calories you are taking in before dieting in order to properly begin your diet. I recommend keeping a food log for 3 days *(Be honest because this will give you a more accurate starting point)*. Track every calorie consumed on these three days. After the 3 days are up take the total number of calories per day and add them together. Then divide that total by 3 so we can get your average calorie intake.

Day 1: 3500 calories

Day 2: 4300 calories

Day 3: 3700 calories

3-day average is 3800 calories.

This is the key part here, in order to lose weight, you need to be in a caloric deficit *(taking in less calories then you burn)* but you do not need to be in a steep caloric deficit. Try starting with a 500-calorie deficit and go from there.

3800 current caloric intake - 500 calorie deficit per day
= 3300 calories to begin your cut

Rule No. 2 - Figure Out Your Macros

Protein - Protein is so important while dieting! Protein provides our bodies with the building blocks we need for muscle. It's commonly recommend for someone trying to drop fat, 1 - 1.25g of protein, per pound of bodyweight... daily.

For our example let's say I weigh 190lbs and I am trying to get to 183lbs for the 83kg class. Bodyweight: 190lbs x 1.25g per pound = 237g *(You can round it up to 240g for simplicity.)*

Fat - Fat is usually the next thing to figure out. I do not like to bring fat below 20% of our total calories. 3300 x.20 = 660 calories from fat / 9 calories per gram = 73g per day

Carbs - Try to keep carb intake as high as possible when trying to lose body fat. Carbohydrates will keep your muscles full and fueled up and also provide you with a feeling of satiety. Use up your remaining calories for carbohydrates.

Total Caloric Goal = 3300

Protein = 240g per day x 4 calories per gram = 960 calories

+

Fat calories = 660

So far: 1620 total calories

Next, take our total calories and subtract that from what you have so far: 3300 – 1620 = 1680 calories from carbs per day. Divide the total by 4 to get total grams of carbs per day = 420g of carbs per day. Done!

Rule No. 3 - Give Yourself Plenty Of Time To Lose The Weight

The worst thing you can do is have to cut calories severally to drop weight into a meet. Take your time dieting so you never really have to drop your calories super low. The goal is to keep your calories as high as possible while still losing around ½ pound per week. By losing slowly, you allow your body to adjust to your new weight and to allow yourself to adjust to any new leverages you may come across. It's commonly recommend to diet for 12-24 weeks before a meet to drop down a weight class. A lifter would rather be lighter, then miss their class and have to compete one class higher.

What To Do If You Reach Your Weight Goal Before The Meet.

This is the ideal situation. If you reach your weight goal before the meet, you can now slowly add calories back into your diet *(reverse dieting)*. A common recommendation for this is 5-10% of your calories every week. By adding calories in you are speeding up your metabolism and giving your body fuel to work with, which will allow you to feel less, drained.

With reverse dieting you do not want to gain weight. You want to add only enough to let you maintain or even lose weight. If you happen to find yourself gaining weight scale down the calories by 20%.

Rule No. 4 - Refeed Twice Per Week

Two days per week (Schedule these days on your hardest workouts for the week), you need to have a "refeed day". Basically we will be taking your calories back up to maintenance. This will give you a mental break and to help restore the fat burning hormones like leptin and T3. Try to raise your daily carb intake by 100g, drop your fat by 5g and drop your protein down by 10g.

Example:

Daily Diet

Protein: 220g
Carbs: 250g
Fat: 55g

Refeed Day:

Protein: 210g

Carbs: 350g

Fat: 50g

Goal # 2 - Gaining Weight To Move Up A Weight Class

Gaining weight seems rather simple, eat more calories than you burn. Remember, you aren't looking to put on any kind of weight. You want to put on lean muscle mass. If you're looking to gain quality muscle you need to follow these basic rules:

Rule No. 1 - Take Your Time

Patience is a virtue. Unfortunately, we all cannot gain 20lbs of true lean mass in a week or two. Despite what the magazines tell you, it's impossible for a natural to do that. I recommend giving yourself plenty of time to gain good quality size. The general rule of thumb for proper lean mass gain is ¼ to ½ pound per week. Giving yourself enough time will ensure you can gain good quality size.

Rule No. 2 - Eat Only 300 Calories Over Your Maintenance

If you are currently taking in around 3300 calories and you are maintaining your weight I would add 300 calories to that to begin your bulk. Since we only synthesize so much muscle in a day, consuming anymore then that will more than likely, make you fat.

Rule No. 3 - If Your Weight Gain Stalls Add Slowly

No need to rush the process as said earlier. If you hit a weight gain plateau, add 100 - 200 calories to your current daily intake and wait at least 2-3 weeks before making a change again. Adding a boatload of calories when you get stuck will just end up making you fat

Rule No. 4 - Keep The Cardio In

I know some of you get excited when it comes to gaining weight because it means you get to stay clear of the cardio machines. Nope, sorry. Cardio while bulking can be beneficial. Cardio can keep you leaner, helping you burn through extra substrates and will also help to improve your endurance.

Goal # 3 - Nutrition For Gym and Meet Day Performance

Gym Performance

Ok so we covered moving up and down in weight classes but what about everyday gym performance. If your performance in the gym sucks, you will end up smaller, risk getting injured, and stand a chance of actually becoming weaker. Your everyday gym performance can make or break you on the platform. If you are not properly fueling your workouts, you won't get anywhere.

Rule #1 - Properly Fuel Each Workout

Consume an adequate number of carbs pre workout. Carbs before workouts fuel your muscle glycogen levels, giving you the energy to perform at maximum level. Keep this meal under 10g of fat so that it doesn't get digested right to your system. It's also recommend to consume 20 - 30g of protein in this meal as well. How many carbs you should eat beforehand, will be determined by what you're trying to do, cut down or bulk up. A general range is 30 - 100g.

Rule No. 2 - Have A Mid-Workout Shake / Bar

Powerlifting training can be brutal. Set after set, rep after rep. Some point in your workout, you will feel totally spent and ready to leave the gym. This is where a mid-workout bar or shake can help give you that extra push you need to finish your workout strong. Trying finding something that has some form of fast digesting carbohydrates and 5g of BCAAs.

If you're cutting, consume 15 - 20g of carbs. If you're bulking, 25 - 35g, depending on your total carb intake. This mid-workout bar /

meal has helped many lifters get thru some brutal workouts. They actually make you give you a boost right when you need it. Some people like to sip this thru their workouts. Some lifters like to start sipping it almost at the point when they feel like they're fading *(usually about an hour into their training)*.

Meet Day Performance

The big day has finally arrived. All your training boils down to the next couple of hours. You want to make sure you're properly fueled. If you have to make weight for a meet, I suggest not eating or drinking until after you weigh in. Once you weigh in, begin sipping water and consume a medium sized meal with around 30g of protein and 50-70g of carbs while staying under 15g of fat.

My coach always recommended something like 1.5 scoops of whey protein mixed with 2 - 3 packets of instant oatmeal, and 1tbsp peanut butter. This meal will digest slow and give you a slow release of glucose into the blood stream. Depending on how long you have between weigh in and your first lift, you may want to consume another 30g of carbs with some fat.

As you begin performing your squat warm ups, try sipping on a caffeine based pre workout mixed with 30-50g of liquid carbs. For a good burst of energy, only consume half this drink while warming up for squats. Consume the other half of this mix after your second attempt on Bench press, to help you have energy to finish strong.

Nutrition is a vital component of strength but it is not the end all be all. You still have to make sure you are training properly. Always strive to consistently add weight to the bar. Doing this over the years, will add up to extremely impressive numbers.

Page Intentionally Left Blank

Chapter 11

Powerlifting For Competition

Fortunately, there is a solution, and it's not performing multiple sets of whatever cable kegel exercise is being pushed as "the answer." Just a little hard, smart, basic work. It's boring, I agree. Do you want to be entertained or get big and strong?

~ Jim Wendler

In a meet, lifts may be performed equipped or un-equipped *(typically referred to as 'raw' lifting or 'classic' in the IPF specifically).* In some federations, knee wraps are permitted in the equipped but not un-equipped division; in others, they may be used in both equipped and un-equipped lifting. Weight belts, knee sleeves, wrist wraps and special footwear may also be used, but are not considered when distinguishing equipped from un-equipped lifting *(in most organizations).*

Powerlifting meets take place across the world. They are mostly commonly found in the United States, Australia, Canada, United Kingdom, Colombia, Iceland, South Africa, Poland, Sweden, Norway, Finland, Russia, Taiwan, Japan and Ukraine. Powerlifting has been a Paralympic sport *(bench press only)* since 1984 and, under the IPF, is also a World Games sport. Local, national and international competitions have also been sanctioned by other federations operating independently of the IPF.

The Difference Between Classes & Categories & Ranks

Weight Classes

Men: 52 kg, 56 kg, 60 kg, 67.5 kg, 75 kg, 82.5 kg, 90 kg, 100 kg, 110 kg, 125 kg, 140 kg, 140 kg+

Women: 44 kg, 48 kg, 52 kg, 56 kg, 60 kg, 67.5 kg, 75 kg, 82.5 kg, 90 kg, 90 kg +

Since the IPF is the most prominent organization, I also need to show their specific classes (as of 2011):

IPF Weight Classes:

Men: up to 53 kg (Sub-Junior/Junior), 59 kg, 66 kg, 74 kg, 83 kg, 93 kg, 105 kg, 120 kg, 120 kg+

Women: up to 43 kg (Sub-Junior/Junior), 47 kg, 52 kg, 57 kg, 63 kg, 72 kg, 84 kg, 84 kg +

Age Categories

This depends on the federation generally, but the averages are as follows:

- 15-18 (Sub-Jr)
- 19-23 (Jr)
- Open (any age)
- Masters (40+)
- Grandmasters (70+)

Specific to the IPF, the following age categories are used:

- Sub-junior (18 and under)
- Junior (19-23)
- Open (24-39)
- Masters 1 (40-49)
- Masters 2 (50-59)
- Masters 3 (60-65)

- Masters 4 (65-70)
- Grandmasters (70+).

Age category is dependent on the year of the participant's birth. For example, if the lifter turns 18 years old in January, he or she is still considered a sub-junior until the end of that calendar year. Other federations typically break the masters categories down to 5-year increments, for example, 40-44, 45-49, 50-54, etc. Some federations also include a sub-master class from 35-39.

Rank and Classification

There are several classifications in powerlifting that determine rank. These typically include Elite, Master, Class I, II, III, IV. The Elite standard is considered to be within the top 1% of competing powerlifters. Several standards exist, including the United States Powerlifting Association classifications, the IPF/USAPL *(single-ply)* classifications, the APF *(multi-ply)* classifications, and the Anti-Drug Athletes United *(ADAU, raw)* classifications. Countries in the former Soviet Union use a somewhat different nomenclature for the top classes, distinguishing among Masters of sport, International Class; Masters of Sport; and Candidates for Master of Sport.

The Master classification should not be confused with the Master age division, which refers to athletes who are at least 40 years old.

Competition Procedures & Practices

A powerlifting competition typically takes place as follows. Each competitor is allowed three to four attempts on each of the squat, bench press, and deadlift, depending on their standing and the organization they are lifting in. The lifter's best valid attempt on each lift counts toward the competition total. For each weight class, the lifter with the highest total wins. If two or more lifters achieve the same total, the lighter lifter ranks above the heavier lifter.

Competitors are judged against other lifters of the same gender, weight class, and age. This helps to ensure that the accomplishments of lifters like Lamar Gant, who has deadlifted 5 times his bodyweight, are recognized alongside those of Benedikt Magnusson, the current All-time deadlift world record holder.

Events

In a Competition, there are three events: bench press, squat, and deadlift. Some variations of this are found at some meets such "push-pull only" meets where lifters only compete in the bench press and deadlift, with the bench press coming first and the deadlift after. Single lift meets are often held, sometimes alongside a normal 3-lift event. This is most common, in the bench press.

At a meet, the events will follow in this order: squat, then bench press, and the deadlift will be the final lift of the meet. If the federation also has an event for strict curls this will normally occur before the squat event.

Chapter 12

Powerlifting Associations

The higher your energy level, the more
efficient your body. The more efficient
your body, the better you feel and the
more you will use your talent to
produce outstanding results.
~ Anthony Robbins

Here is a list of 13 international federations. They are in alphabetical order. A person should research these entities on their own, and choose one that feels most like "home" to them. I have a great amount of respect for the men & women that own and operate all 13 of these organizations.

1. American Drug Free Powerlifting Federation - adfpf.net
2. Global Powerlifting Committee - worldgpc.com

3. Global Powerlifting Federation - gpfederation.net

4. International Powerlifting Federation (IPF) - powerlifting-ipf.com

5. International Powerlifting League (IPL) – powerlifting-ipl.com

6. Natural Athlete Strength Association – NASA - nasa-sports.com

7. United States Powerlifting Association - uspa.net

8. USA Powerlifting - usapowerlifting.com

9. World Drug-Free Powerlifting Federation - wdfpf.co.uk

10. World Natural Powerlifting Federation - wnpfpl.com

11. World Powerlifting Alliance - apa-wpa.com

12. World Powerlifting Congress - worldpowerliftingcongress.com

13. World Powerlifting Federation - wpfpowerlifting.com

Of these federations, the oldest and most prominent is the IPF. It comprises federations from over 100 countries located on six continents. The IPF is the federation responsible for coordinating participation in the World Games, an international event affiliated with the International Olympic Committee.

The IPF has many affiliates, one of these being USAPL. Specifically, the USAPL regulates all ages of lifters from the high school level to ages 40+ within the United States. The next oldest federation is the WPC, formed as the international companion to the APF after its split from the USPF.

Different federations have different rules and different interpretations of the rules, leading to a myriad of variations. Differences arise on the equipment eligible, clothing, drug testing and aspects of allowable technique. The 100% Raw Federation allows no supportive gear to be worn by the lifter while the IPF, AAU, NASA, USAPL and the ADFPF only allow a single-ply tight polyester squat suit, deadlift suit and bench shirt, wraps for knees and wrists, and a belt in the equipped divisions.

Other federations, such as the APF, APA, IPA, SPF, WPC, AWPC and WPO, allow opened or closed back bench shirts, multi-ply gear, and a wide array of gear materials such as canvas, denim, polyester etc.

The IPF has suspended entire member nations' federations, including the Russian Federation, Ukraine, Kazakhstan, Iran, India and Uzbekistan, for repeated violations of the IPF's anti-doping policies. So, they obviously take things very seriously!

Page Intentionally Left Blank

Chapter 13

Powerlifting For Women

There's more to life than training, but
training is what puts more in your life.
~ Brooks Kubik

There are many workouts marketed specifically toward women: Pilates, Zumba, Barre, Yoga, etc. None of these are bad workouts necessarily, but if you ask me, there's one workout style that really shines for women, you guessed it… powerlifting. Previously a male-dominated workout, women are discovering powerlifting and fueling an explosion of participation in the sport.

11 Reasons Why Powerlifting Is An Awesome Sport For Women

1. Most Women Have Plenty Of Flexibility & Few Have Adequate Strength.

   a. Yoga is great for stretching, and Zumba is terrific for cardio, but powerlifting will make you strong. Yes, it really is possible to strengthen your entire body with just three lifts. The squat works your legs, butt, abs, and back; the bench press hits your chest, shoulders, and arms; the deadlift works your legs, butt, and abs again, but also your back, shoulders, and arms.

b. Building strength makes everything else more effective. Adding strength to your body supercharges your stretching and cardio — even your metabolism! That means you can actually eat more calories while maintaining a healthy weight.

2. It Satisfies Your Competitive Drive.

a. Many women talk about how they enjoy competition, but don't always like it in the gym. They don't want to look at the person next to them in a workout and feel like a drag racer revving their engine. Powerlifting is a competitive outlet, but the competition is truly within yourself. You're working to be the strongest version of yourself, and you might just win a gnarly trophy while you're at it.

3. It Is Quantifiably Empowering.

    a. Many female fitness hobbyists reveal that they get very frustrated, when they don't have a reliable sense of whether they're making progress toward their fitness goals. That leaves only subjectivity, which is problematic because the way you perceive your body can change day-to-day and can ultimately lead you on a roller coaster of emotions.

    b. Powerlifting is concerned with hard data - easily trackable numbers, indicators of your strength - that you can see improve dramatically over a short period of time. A woman might start out deadlifting 50-70 pounds, and after a few months, can safely and easily deadlift 200 pounds. If that seems like an extreme number to you, you probably don't realize how strong women really are.

    c. I've lost track of how many women in my gym can deadlift over 200 pounds. It's an extraordinary feeling to see those abilities increase. If you start out being able to squat 65 pounds for five reps, then you can do 95 pounds for 10 reps, there can be no mistake: you are stronger. The numbers don't lie.

4. It Offers An Athletic Physique.

    a. I don't think that there's anything wrong with training for looks. I saw a meme the other day that said "Skinny people look ok in clothes but strong people look amazing naked!" I'll just leave that there.

    b. Powerlifting gives women athletic legs, buoyant buttocks, sculpted shoulders, and toned arms. Plus, the supercharged metabolism makes it easier to burn fat, should you want to do that, too. Whatever your goal for your physique, powerlifting can help move you in the right direction.

5. You Can Start Today!

    a. You don't need any special equipment, other than what your gym already has. It doesn't matter how in or out-of-shape you are. With just a little instruction in how to do the lifts properly and a beginner's template, you can begin training in powerlifting today.

    b. Powerlifting is flexible; you can focus on your strength for a few months, then take those gains and apply them to other workouts, or, if you really catch the bug, you can keep powerlifting indefinitely. You will never run out of weight to lift, and you will never tire of growing stronger.

6. It's A Huge Relief To Stop Thinking About Your Physique Constantly

    a. Maybe a bit contrary to number 4 above, but that's ok. In powerlifting, we focus on numbers! That's it. As I mentioned earlier, I don't subscribe to the attitude that sometimes surfaces in the female strength training media (whether it's intentional or not) that just wanting to look good naked is somehow a lesser goal than pursuing strength.

    b. But many women have said… one of their favorite things about powerlifting was that focusing so intently on their numbers allowed them to completely forget about their physique for months on end. After their workouts, they found themselves basking in new personal records rather than scoping themselves out in the mirror, to see if their butt was finally getting bigger.

7. Your Physique Will Not Suffer *(It Will Probably Improve)*

    a. To piggy back on numbers 4 & 6, remember - lifting heavy won't make a woman bulky – it'll actually help you get leaner and more defined.

    b. Losing body fat is the last thing many women expect to happen when they start powerlifting. They notice that their legs are leaner and so are the backs of their arms!

    c. To put things bluntly:

        i. Powerlifting + Shitty Diet = "Powerlifting makes you fat"

        ii. Powerlifting + Sound Nutrition = "Powerlifting makes you hot & sexy"

8. It Will Improve Your Relationship With Food

    a. There's something inherently different about the way you see food when you're training to look good, compared to when you're training to set personal records.

    b. Powerlifting reinforces the message "food is a fuel that can help your body perform" and not just a means to an end to make you look a certain way.

9. You Will Feel Like A Super Hero

    a. In the grand scheme of things, you may find there are much stronger people out there in the world. Who cares? Powerlifting is about your numbers! That's it! And it feels, amazing! It's amazing what you can accomplish, if you just keep plugging away at something, day after day.

10. You ARE Strong Enough

    a. People are always running road races "just to have something to train for", or "just to get in shape" and with no particular goal other than "just to finish." You can do that with powerlifting too, and (in my very biased opinion) you'll have a lot more fun!

    b. It's not important that you're strong compared to other people, only that you're strong for you. One of my favorite things about powerlifting is that it truly is a competition against yourself and your own personal records. You might find though, that by the time the meet comes around you ended up a lot stronger than you thought you would.

11. It Will Inspire Other Women

    a. So many female lifters have stated something like, "I never would have considered powerlifting if I hadn't seen other women do it first." The more women there are who powerlift, the more women there will be who realize that they can do it also.

Chapter 14

Powerlifting For Children

That's the beauty of coaching. You get to touch lives, you get to make a difference. You get to do things for people who will never pay you back and they say you never have had a perfect day until you've done something for someone who will never pay you back.

~Morgan Wootten

When working with kids, the actual planning and implementation of a training program requires much more consideration than we sometimes give to our own training cycles. You are responsible for that youth, and you will be the first one the parents of that young person will blame, if something happens to their child.

The first two questions that pop into the minds of parents when they realize their baby prefers dumbbells to soccer balls are "Is it safe for kids to lift weights?" and "At what age can kids start lifting weights?" The sad truth is there are many doubts surround the safety and validity of weight training for children. Many would even have you believe that kids have no place at all in the weight room. Despite this belief, exercise physiologists and the American Academy of Pediatrics both support the implementation of strength and resistance training programs, for young children.

Is It Safe For Kids To Lift Weights?

The answer from today's top research authorities is a resounding "yes." Studies show that a moderate intensity strength training program can help increase strength, decrease the risks of injury while playing other sports, increase motor performance skills and increase bone density, and enhance growth and development in children. Exercise physiologists aren't the only ones recommending resistance training; the American Academy of Pediatrics has also put forth a pro-strength training for children statement.

The American Academy of Pediatrics position on strength training supports the implementation of strength and resistance training programs, even for prepubescent children that are monitored by well-trained adults and take into account the child's maturation level. The only limitation the AAP suggests is to avoid repetitive maximal lifts *(lifts that are one repetition maximum lifts or are within 2-3 repetitions of a one repetition maximum lift)* until they have reached the level of developmental maturity in which visible secondary sex characteristics have been developed. Also, it's in this stage that adolescents will also have passed their period of maximal velocity of height growth. However, there is some evidence that one-repetition maximal testing can be safely administered IF proper technique has been mastered.

The AAP's concern that children wait until this stage to perform maximal lifts is that the epiphyses, commonly called "growth plates", are still very vulnerable to injury before this developmental stage. It is repeated injury to these growth plates that may hinder growth. However, more recently, several studies have been conducted that show that the risk of these types of injuries occur LESS during weight training compared to other sports. In fact, in published literature, all incidences of injury were attributed to either poor training design or lack of supervision.

At What Age Can Kids Start Lifting Weights?

Neither the AAP or exercise physiologists have a minimum age set for a child to begin a resistance training program. Research has been done on moderate weight training programs with children as young as 4 years. However, care should be taken in the progression of a program.

The first objective of a training program is to introduce the body to the stresses of training and to teach basic technique and form, not the amount of weight used. Light weight training can be introduced in order to establish a foundation. Many coaches recommend a training scheme of 10 - 15 repetitions and 1 - 3 sets per muscle group. The weight should be one that the child can lift for 10 - 15 repetitions without going to muscular failure.

Once a base has been established, the amount of exercises and the weight lifted can be increased and a more advanced routine can be incorporated. It is important to note that there is no real time frame for this progression. Children will advance on a very individual basis, and it is up to you as a coach to recognize good skill and technique and hence the ability to safely increase the weights lifted.

You may be questioning the use of higher reps for children compared to adult powerlifters. There is actually a very good reason why higher reps should be used for prepubescent lifters. Before puberty, the majority of strength gains are neurological in nature. That is, initial strength gains do not come from muscle hypertrophy as they do in adults. Think of a higher rep scheme as a blueprint for what is to come. *Higher reps allow children to build a physiological pathway for their technique.*

It is appropriate to very gradually increase the volume and intensity. Despite recent progress in the research of resistance training and children, there is still not enough information to make safe assumptions about percentage-based progressions that are often used in higher-level programs.

Care should also be taken when performing one-repetition maximum testing. In a recent study that investigated maximal strength testing in children, the researchers needed 7 to 11 sets to determine a one-repetition maximum, as opposed to the normal 3 to 5 used in adult tests.

Tips for Supervising a Youth Strength Training Program

Safety should always come first when training a youth or child. It is helpful to prepare yourself for any and all possibilities. Preparation is also helpful in easing the minds on concerned parents. Below are some helpful tips that will help to ensure the safety of your young charges.

1. Before you begin training anyone under the age of 18, be sure to have written parental and medical permission to do so. This consent form should also include a disclosure of all known medical conditions that you should be aware about. If there are any conditions, such as diabetes or asthma, make sure you are fully informed about emergency procedures.

2. Make sure the equipment you will be using is free from defects. Also be aware that the equipment is adequate for young children, who may not be able to lift a normal 45-pound bar or may not be tall enough to use the squat racks or bench.

3. It is vitally important that young lifters are adequately hydrated and have had at least a small meal within a few hours of training.

4. Athletes should be sufficiently warmed-up before beginning a training session.

5. Youth should always be under the direct supervision of a competent trainer or coach when weight training.

6. Employ a wide variety of exercises and training styles to keep interest levels high and encourage participation in a wide variety of sports and activities.

7. You should have personal liability insurance in case of an accident. Depending on your circumstance, you may need to get a personal training certification from a reputable organization to obtain this. If you are working in a school or a gym, be sure to ask if their coverage covers you.

8. Make sure that the environment is conducive to training. If you are training in a gym that doesn't have air-conditioning in the middle of a heat wave, take special precautions to ensure that everyone is staying hydrated. If possible, train in the morning when it is cooler, and don't be afraid to cancel squat day if the temperature is too high.

   a. Weather reporters sometimes use the term "wet-bulb globe temperature," especially in the summer. In hot weather, it is advantageous to pay attention to this number. The National Athletic Trainer's Association recommends that training or events be delayed if this temperature reaches 82 degrees. Keep in mind this is the wet-bulb globe temperature, not what we normally consider the "temperature" to be. A wet-bulb globe temperature of 73° *(which is a high-risk level)* is approximately the same as a dry-bulb temperature *("normal" temperature)* of 73° with 100% humidity and a dry-bulb temperature of 93° at 20% humidity.

9. Be able to provide informational sources to parents of young lifters to erase and lingering doubts they have about their children lifting weights. This will also be helpful educating the parents about the importance of instilling health lifestyle choices at a young age. Coaches often have no control over the eating habits, sleeping patterns, etc of

their athletes, so communication with the parents is vital to enhance these very important ideals.

Following these basic guidelines will help develop safe and effective programs for young children and adolescents. However, there are certainly many other considerations that will be specific to your program. For instance, if you are training adolescents who are Muslim, it is important to ask if they take part in Ramadan, a month long period of fasting during daylight hours. If they do, you will need to make adjustments to the intensity of their training and possibly time of the day they train at.

As a final reminder, because this cannot be stressed enough, at all times remember that children should progress at their own pace. Though this makes training difficult in a school or club setting, because training program will have to be individualized, it is incredibly important to insure the health and safety of your athletes. It is also important to stay aware of the current of research in this growing field. The following are a few references to help you plan and implement a training program for young kids.

1. Strength Training for Young Athletes by Fleck and Kraemer. This book can be obtained through any online bookstore such as Amazon.com or Borders.com. It is very user friendly for those who don't have an extensive background in exercise science.

2. The National Strength and Conditioning Association's Position Statement on Youth Resistance Training. This can be obtained for a small fee from:

   a. nsca-lift.org/Publications/posstatements.shtml

3. Developmental Exercise Physiology by Rowland. This book goes into all aspects of fitness for children, and offers explanations for physiological responses for children. I would recommend it for those who want a little more explanation as to the science behind exercise and children.

4. Roundtable Discussion: Youth Resistance Training. This article is found in the Strength and Conditioning Journal, Volume 26, number 1, pages 49-64. You can order just this article from:

   a. nsca.allenpress.com/nscaonline/?request=index-html

Let's Pretend We've Been Given A New Youth To Train

First, we need to get our head & ego in line. If your idea of introducing a kid to weight training is to have him follow you around and do whatever you do, you're bound to crush his spirit *(along with his body)*. Remember, a simple 3-day-a-week bodyweight program, will habituate them to the idea that we train Monday, Wednesday, and Saturday, every single week. The coolest thing about helping to guide a youngster into the weight room and getting them started is that, if you do a good job, it's something they could be doing for the next 50 years.

Phase One: Bodyweight-only Exercises

The goal here is to take a high school age *(14 - 18 year old)* non-athlete and get them started in the training world. That means teaching them the basics of how, what, and why, while also helping them build a strong and healthy body.

If the personal trainer's Golden Rule is "Do no harm," that concept becomes infinitely more pronounced when it comes to training teens. When motivation, enthusiasm, and unchecked ego meet new movement patterns, uncertain capabilities, and loaded barbells, things can go catastrophic in an instant.

The most effective way to introduce young lifters to training is by starting with a well-designed bodyweight routine. It allows you to build a base level of strength, muscular coordination/body awareness, and conditioning. Some muscular size is also a very welcomed side effect.

Not only do bodyweight exercises promote inter-muscular coordination and balance better than free weights *(if a kid can't do a few good bodyweight squats, you're not going to want to put a 45-pound bar on his back)*, they also lend themselves to what author, Tudor Bompa called, *anatomical adaptation*, or AA.

AA is a period of relatively higher-rep training designed to physically prepare a new or deconditioned lifter for an intense lifting program. AA is used to develop the tendons, ligaments, and smaller support structures before progressing to heavier, lower rep, higher intensity training.

This type of routine also builds the habit of, "We train on Monday, Wednesday, and Saturday, every single week", while introducing our beginner to the muscular fatigue and, to an extent, soreness that they'll come to know and love.

Their First Three Days a Week Routine

Exercise	Sets	Reps
Bodyweight Squat	2	12 - 15
Push-Up	2	12 - 15
Bodyweight Alternating Lunge	2	12 - 15 per leg
Neutral-Grip Pull-Up	2	12 - 15
or Horizontal Row		

Exercise	Sets	Reps
Plank	2	15 - count
Burpees	2	15

It might look simple, but it's plenty to start with, as long as you reinforce proper technique for each rep and don't rush through each set.

On squats, the feet should stay flat the entire time, not buckling up on the toes or back on the heels. Push-ups are done on the toes, legs straight, going through a full range of motion. Raise the hands onto a bench to make them easier, if necessary. The lunges alternate legs each rep, but make sure the hips are moving "up and down" more than "front and back."

Use bands to assist on the pull-ups if necessary or use the Smith machine for horizontal rows as an alternative. The neutral-grip *(aka straight grip)* incorporates the most arm work and puts the lifter in the strongest pulling position.

The plank is the easiest of the bunch, simply holding the top part of a push-up with super-strict posture from neck to ankles. And the 4-count burpee *(no jump needed)* ends the session with a bit of everything – a little cardio, a little flexibility, "hidden" plank work, and "hidden" squat work.

One key concept, possibly the most important concept when it comes to kids and lifting, is to avoid muscular failure. Remember that from earlier in the chapter? Every single set should be ended well-before true failure is reached, ideally keeping one or two reps with good technique "in the tank."

Old school lifters' mentality might be to continue each set until the bar doesn't move an inch. However, when it comes to young adults and their still-developing bodies, if the target muscle has reached failure, the undeveloped support structures around that muscle have been pushed beyond failure and the youth is now at risk of legitimate injury.

This is the one and only aspect of lifting that the old *"weight training stunts children's growth"* myth has any bearing on. While supervised, well-designed training programs are absolutely beneficial to kids, a poorly designed and/or poorly supervised program can be equally damaging.

Avoiding muscular failure should be the number-one underlying theme in any young lifter's program until he's nearing the end of puberty *(or past 18 years old as a very general rule of thumb)*. And even then, it's debatable whether or not training up to or beyond failure is necessary for anyone.

Phase Two: Hitting The Gym

Once the youth has built a fair amount of strength, conditioning, and patience with bodyweight work, they're ready to advance to the weight room. This allows more focus on the powerlifting movements and teaching them to focus on their numbers.

The simplest routine to start with, is one lift... per day. For example, *Monday* = Squat | *Wednesday* = Bench Press | *Friday* = Deadlift. Week one should involve no more than two sets. We're not trying to make them sore. We're trying to create proper form, provide ample recovery time, and build a habit. Finally, having a training notebook also makes it easier, since the exercise names and technique notes can be written in as you go along.

Kid's Nutrition and Supplements

Youth need to be taught that "Bodybuilding is 75% nutrition," or "Results are 90% nutrition,". You choose, but the message is all the same.

Just like avoiding muscle failure is crucial to lifting, if there's one idea that should run through every young lifter's nutrition plan, it's that *they are not little bodybuilders*. They're still developing and, as such, they need plenty of quality food.

"Cutting" and "bulking" aren't at all relevant to their situation. Sure, if a kid's a bit heavier and wants to lean up, he'll eat less than a skinny kid trying to gain weight. But they need to develop smart, well-balanced, healthy eating habits that encourage recovery and growth. Save any thoughts of bulking and cutting for long after they've established a foundation.

We want to keep things simple with practical, easy-to-follow guidelines. Kids who lift should be eating at least three meals a day, seven days a week. Skipping meals means skipping results.

Again: Skipping meals means skipping results.

On top of those three meals, you could add one protein shake per day, plus a basic workout shake on lifting days. Once a kid is lifting four or more days per week and eating three meals a day seven days a week, then they could add in something like creatine. Regardless, keep supplements to an absolute minimum and focus on eating good food.

Protein Sources

1. Farm animals: Chicken breast or thigh, steak, ground beef, ground turkey, pork.
2. Whole eggs, not egg whites. Egg whites are for pre-contest bodybuilders and you're not one, yet.

3. Water animals: Any fish (tuna, salmon, tilapia, etc.), shrimp.

4. Dairy: Milk, cottage cheese, any cheese, Greek yogurt.

5. Sandwich meats: Roast beef, ham, turkey. Not bologna.

Carb Sources

1. White or brown rice

2. High-fiber bread (not white)

3. Oatmeal, cream of wheat, cream of rice

4. Quinoa. Sounds fancy, but it's a "grain" with some protein that cooks like rice.

5. Potatoes: Yellow, white, red, russet, or sweet.

6. Corn

7. Beans. More like red, black, pinto, or kidney, not plain old "baked beans."

8. Fruit. Fruit is awesome, so eat it. Just remember that, nutrition-wise, it's strictly carbs.

9. Vegetables. Again, vegetables are awesome, so eat them.

Fat Sources

1. Olive oil

2. Coconut oil

3. Butter *(real butter, not margarine)*

4. Avocado

5. Nuts: Walnuts, almonds, cashews, other nuts and any butters made from them.

6. Any fats found naturally in your protein sources: Fish oil, fat in red meat, fat in dairy, etc.

A combo of those three categories should make up a large majority of the kid's diet, but if he has some soda, candy, or other 100% certifiable junk food once in a while, it's not the end of the world.

Yes, we're trying to build a healthy lifestyle, but telling a young kid to avoid "bad food" all day every day, is impractical for a teenager and is almost guaranteed to make him the outcast of whatever social group he fits into.

If you want to take their nutrition up another level, get them familiar with three essential techniques in the kitchen – cooking scrambled eggs, making hard-boiled eggs, and cooking some chicken or meat in a pan. Figuring out those three things can help them be pretty self-sufficient for a good deal of their daily protein.

We could talk about the studies showing the connection between exercise and improved classroom performance, or we could talk about how a well-designed training plan can get him onto a team, improve him as an athlete, and eventually give him an edge over his teammates and his opponents.

But at the end of the day, the coolest thing about helping to guide a young person into the weight room and getting them started is that, if you do a good job, it's something they could be doing for the next 50 years. And you were a part of that! That's pretty awesome.

More Ideas Supporting Powerlifting For Kids

The three main powerlifts - the squat, bench press and deadlift - along *with* the strict curl, develop overall body strength. Strength is a very important factor in a majority of sports. It makes sense that many coaches encourage their lifters to participate in a powerlifting oriented training program. In addition, the powerlifts, when combined with a healthy diet, are very effective at adding muscle mass to the body. The additional muscle mass is not only useful in sports, particularly for high school athletes whom are often lighter than they desire to be, but it may help build their confidence as well.

But Is It Really Safe? Like Mentioned Earlier In The Book?

To assess how likely a sport is to cause injury to the participant, sports and activities are given injury rates per 100 hours of participation. Below is a chart that includes sample sports and their injury rating. As you can see, weight lifting is very safe compared to basically any sport, it is even safer than gym class.

Sport/Activity	Rate of Injury per 100 hrs
Youth Soccer	6.2000
Basketball	1.0200
Physical Education Class	0.1800
Weight Lifting	0.0012

Chart Is From: Starting Strength, Rippetoe and Kilgore, 2005

Many strength and condition professionals feel that a proper strength training program will significantly *decrease the risk of injury* because weight lifting strengthens not only the muscles but the bones, ligaments, joints, and connective tissue in the body. A body in good shape is much less likely to get injured than a body that is deconditioned.

If you are searching for a qualified instructor to teach these lifts and others to your child look for someone who is certified by the National Personal Training Institute (NPTI) or someone that has the "Starting Strength Coaching" Certification.

As previously mentioned, lifting weights is generally safe but that does not mean that it does not pose any chance of injury. *It is strongly suggested that all high school students (and younger) lift in a supervised setting with qualified instruction.* In addition, it is very important that the athletes have proper form on the exercises at all times. It can be very tempting for high school students, particularly competitive males, to want to lift more than their friends. This can lead to them making large jumps in weight and allowing their form to break down to temporarily lift more weight. This needs to be avoided.

Exercises that work the primary joints of the body *(shoulders and hips)* needed to be performed with strict form, particularly those that place a load on the lower back *(squats and deadlifts)*. Student athletes need to take the time to learn the movements correctly before weight is added, and periodically the form should be reevaluated to see if any flaws have emerged.

If an athlete experiences pain in a joint they should immediately stop the exercise and see if the instructor can evaluate their form as they perform the exercise with light weight. Generally, corrections in form will cause any pain to go away, but if the athlete cannot perform the exercise pain free then the weight should be severely reduced… or the exercise should not be performed and a substitute exercise should be given.

Additional Benefits of Powerlifting for Kids

Powerlifting offers many health benefits such as stronger muscles, stronger bones *(and a decreased chance of developing osteoporosis later in life)*, stronger joints, improved metabolism, improved body composition *(lose fat and gain muscle)*, improved work capacity, and a decreased risk of developing type II diabetes *(which is becoming more and more common in children and teens)*. In addition, Powerlifting and weight lifting doesn't have to stop when high school ends.

Most high school athletes will not continue to play to competitive sports in college, and even fewer college athletes will play professional sports. But lifting weights is a viable form of exercise for those of any age. Powerlifting in specific, has age groups. As mentioned earlier in the book, there are groups for those under 13, 14-15, 16-17, 18-19, 20-24, 25-39, and then once you get into the master's category (over 40) you can continue to lift as an adult. Females are also encouraged to compete in powerlifting during the years of puberty and beyond. It's particularly important for young women to help develop good bone strength. *(In addition to the many reasons stated in the prior chapter.)*

Aside from improved sport performance, powerlifting can offer teens many different benefits. Lifting weights is a unique activity, in that it is very objective *(you either lifted the weight or you did not)*. It is extremely easy to see if improvement is being made *(either more weight was lifted, more reps were performed, or you handled the same weight but with much more control & stability)*. This provides continuous feedback to the athlete about their training.

In an ideal world, difficult but achievable goals are set, the athlete works hard towards those goals and achieves them, and a sense of accomplishment is felt. Continued success in the gym and on the field should lead to a sense of personal confidence that hopefully can be applied in many situations in life, including school and work.

Powerlifting can be a very valuable, healthy addition to your child's life, whether it involves participation for 3 months or 10 years. *It reinforces the benefits of a good work ethic and a healthy lifestyle.* It fosters *discipline* and *patience* as the gains don't come over night. Exercise has also been shown to improve concentration levels, the ability to focus on one task, and a general sense of well-being. With your support your student athlete may improve their sporting performance and they may possibly find another activity which will *add to their overall happiness and fulfillment.*

If you are interested in finding out more information about powerlifting, especially for teens, here is the NSCA position statement of weight training for youths:

nsca-lift.org/Publications/YouthforWeb.pdf

Chapter 15

Hall Of Champions

Your love for what you do and willingness to
push yourself where others aren't prepared to go
is what will make you great.

~ Laurence Shahlaei

On the next couple of pages, I've listed a small sample of world record lifts. These lifts were achieved in RAW / Unequipped meets. For the men, I've listed couple of the lightest athletes... and a couple of the heaviest. For the women, I've listed a few from the middle weight-range lifters. The men results were pulled from drug-tested meets. For the women records, I wasn't able to determine whether or not drug testing was done. One thing you'll notice, is that the lighter athletes tend to be pound-for-pound, stronger than the heaviest athletes. Anyway, review & enjoy.

Bodyweight Class	Amount Lifted	Athlete	Date

Mens Squat

SHW	966	Ray Williams	06/26/16
308	859	M. Bouafia Alg	10/11/14
132	551	Mike Booker	2002
123	639	Andrzej Stanaszek	05/09/02

Mens Bench Press

SHW	710	James Henderson	1997
308	633	Steve Wong	11/18/02
148	498	Lei liu	06/02/12
132	462	Sherif Othman	03/16/15
123	455	Sheriff Othman	02/23/12

Bodyweight Class	Amount Lifted	Athlete	Date

Mens Deadlift

Bodyweight Class	Amount Lifted	Athlete	Date
SHW	903	Mark Henry	1995
308	939	K. K. Latvia	2009
132	602	Sergey Fedosienko	5/30/15
123	562	Sergey Fedosienko	2009

Womens Squat

Bodyweight Class	Amount Lifted	Athlete	Date
114	340	Jenn Rotsinger	11/08/14
123	369	Inna Filimonova	06/01/14
132	451	M. Gasparyan	11/12/14
148	450	Rheta West	10/06/12

Womens Bench Press

Bodyweight Class	Amount Lifted	Athlete	Date
114	288	Esther Oyema	09/01/12
123	315	Fatma Omar	09/02/12
132	300	Jennifer Thompson	03/02/12
148	325	Souhad Ghazouani	07/28/10

Bodyweight Class	Amount Lifted	Athlete	Date

Womens Deadlift

Bodyweight Class	Amount Lifted	Athlete	Date
114	408	Jenn Rotsinger	08/25/13
123	454	Janis Finkleman	08/02/15
132	485	Susan Salazar	11/07/15
148	529	Julia Zaugolova	06/30/12

Chapter 16

Conclusion

You may encounter many defeats, but you must not be defeated. In fact, it may be necessary to encounter the defeats, so you can know who you are, what you can rise from, how you can still come out of it.

~ Maya Angelou

The above quote by Maya Angelou is a powerful lesson. It applies not only to powerlifting, but to any great goal, and life itself. In the beginning of the book I told you my goal was to "sell you" on powerlifting. I hope I've done that. If I haven't, I appreciate the time that you've invested reading this book, and at least considering it.

Powerlifting has been a blessing in my life, as well as millions of other athletes around the globe. I wish you the very best!

Page Intentionally Left Blank

Resources

Here are my three favorite websites relating to powerlifting:

1. **Bodybuilding.com** – Yes, the name… I know. Trust me. This site has amazing educational information. In addition, their exercise demonstration videos are excellent!

2. **PowerliftingToWin.com**

3. **PowerliftingWatch.com**

Page Intentionally Left Blank

About the Author

Brian K. Allen has been involved with strength training for over 25 years. His need for strength training is mostly a result of his career. He's been an executive protection agent *(bodyguard)* almost his entire adult life.

He is not a competitive powerlifter, yet he recommends powerlifting to everyone! He hopes that people who've never even considered this activity, will somehow see this book... and become involved.

Page Intentionally Left Blank

Earn The Title Of:

Powerlifting Coach & Referee

Online!

If you'd like to enhance your professionalism, update your resume, and gain a marketing edge *(if you train clients as a business)*, then our course may be just what you're looking for.

Visit our website today, and request the FREE course module that is available. We look forward to assisting you with your professional development.

InternationalPowerliftersCouncil.com

Page Intentionally Left Blank

Made in the USA
Middletown, DE
10 November 2017